Heinemann STATE STUDIES

All Around Illinois

Regions and Resources

Andrew Santella

Heinemann Library
Chicago, Illinois

© 2003, 2008 Heinemann Library
a division of Reed Elsevier Inc.
Chicago, Illinois
Customer Service 888-454-2279

Visit our website at **www.heinemannlibrary.com**

Designed by Kimberly R. Miracle and Betsy Wernert
Printed and bound in the United States by Lake Book Manufacturing, Inc

12 11 10 09 08
10 9 8 7 6 5 4 3 2 1

New edition ISBNs: 978-1-4329-0267-4 (hardcover)
                   978-1-4329-0274-2 (paperback)

The Library of Congress cataloged the first edition as follows:
Santella, Andrew.
  All around Illinois : regions and resources / by Andrew Santella.
      p. cm. -- (State studies)
Includes bibliographical references and index.
  ISBN 1-4034-0007-5 (HC), 1-4034-0568-9 (Pbk)
  1. Illinois--Geography--Juvenile literature.
  [1. Illinois--Geography.] I. Title. II. State studies (Heinemann Library (Firm))
  F541.8 .S26 2002
  917.73--dc21
                        2002000795

Acknowledgments
The author and publishers are grateful to the following for permission to reproduce copyright material:

Cover photography reproduced with permission of Superstock/Dwight Ellefsen.

pp. 4, 22, 24, 26, 35B ©Robert Lifson/Heinemann Library; **pp. 5, 8, 11, 13, 16, 19, 21, 29, 30, 37, 39** ©maps.com/ Heinemann Library; **p. 6** ©Bob and Ira Spring/Stock Connection/Picture Quest; **pp. 7, 14, 17, 18, 44** ©James P. Rowan; **p. 9** ©Heinemann Library; **p. 10** ©Ben Weddle/Midwestock; **p. 12B** ©Sandy Felsenthal/Corbis; **p. 12T** ©Charles Rex Arbogast/AP Photo; **p. 15** ©Robert Glusic/Getty Images; **p. 20** ©Don Smetzer; **pp. 23B, 25, 35T, 36** ©Illinois Department of Commerce and Community Affairs; **pp. 23T, 33** ©Milt Mann/Cameramann International; **p. 27** ©Duane Zehr/Bradley University; **p. 28** ©U.S Army Corps of Engineers; **p. 31** ©Tom Sistak/The Daily Times/AP Photo; **p. 32** ©Deere & Company; **p. 34** ©Layne Kennedy/Corbis; **p. 38** ©AP/Wide World Photos; **p. 40** ©Richard Day/Daybreak Imagery; **p. 41** ©Kim Karpeles/Midwestock; **p. 42T** ©Robert Glusic/PhotoDisc; **p. 43T** ©Charles Rex Arbogast/AP Photo; **p. 43B** ©Granite City Division, National Steel Corporation; **p. 45** ©Grant Heilman Photography

Special thanks to Tom Schwartz of the Illinois Historic Preservation Agency, for his expert help and advice on the series.

Every effort has been made to contact copyright holders of any material reproduced in this book. Any omissions will be rectified in subsequent printings if notice is given to the publisher.

Contents

Some words are shown in bold, **like this**. You can find out what they mean by looking in the glossary.

An Introduction to Illinois

Anyone who has taken a trip across Illinois knows most of the state is flat. Fields of corn and soybeans stretch along roads as far as the eye can see. Those crops have helped feed the world for more than 150 years.

However, there is much more to Illinois than flat farmland. Illinois is 385 miles (620 kilometers) long and 218 miles (351 kilometers) wide. Within its borders, a person can find hills, valleys, forests, and **wetlands**. Illinois is bordered by one of the largest lakes in the world, Lake Michigan. It is also home to smaller lakes, both artificial, or human-made, and natural. The state contains tiny country towns and the huge city of Chicago. It supports both farms and factories. Even the weather varies greatly from northern to southern Illinois. It is a state filled with surprises and variety.

Until the mid—1800s, Illinois was mostly prairie land. Today, most of that prairie land has been turned into farm fields of corn and soybeans.

Illinois

Northern

This map shows some of Illinois's main cities and towns.

Galena
Byron
Rockford
Waukegan
Arlington Heights
Des Plaines
Evanston
Elgin
Skokie
Wheaton
Oak Park
Chicago
Dixon
Aurora
Naperville
Tampico
Joliet
Illinois & Michigan Canal
Rock Island
Moline
La Salle
Bishop Hill
Kankakee
Galesburg
Peoria
Eureka
Pekin
Normal
Nauvoo
Bloomington
Danville
Champaign
Urbana

Central

Quincy
Springfield
Arthur
New Salem
Lake Shelbyville
Mattoon
Effingham
Godfrey
Vandalia
Alton
Edwardsville
Collinsville
Carlyle Lake
East St. Louis
Centralia
Cahokia
Mt. Vernon
Grayville
Prairie du Rocher
Rend Lake
Kaskaskia
Shawneetown
Carbondale

Southern

Cairo

Fox River
Mississippi River
Rock River
Kankakee River
Illinois River
Sangamon River
Illinois River
Kaskaskia River
Embarras River
Wabash River
Mississippi River
Big Muddy River
Ohio River

N
W   E
S

0   50 miles
0   50 km

Glacier-made

Much of Illinois was shaped by **glaciers**. Glaciers are huge sheets of ice that can cover hundreds of miles of land and be over a mile thick. One hundred thousand years ago, glaciers began spreading south over Illinois. They covered almost all of the state. Fifteen thousand years ago, the glaciers began melting in a northerly direction.

When the glaciers disappeared they left behind a changed land. The glaciers were so heavy that they had flattened much of Illinois. Only the areas that were not covered by glaciers were not flattened, such as the northwest corner of the state. Today, rolling hills rise along the rivers there. Illinois's highest point is in Jo Daviess County. It's called Charles Mound, and it is 1,235 feet (376 meters) tall.

Thousands of years ago, glaciers similar to this one (left) helped shape the Illinois land. Glaciers can be as much as a mile thick, but usually only move about 12 inches (30.5 centimeters) a day.

The Mississippi River (above) forms the western border of Illinois. People have traveled up and down the mighty Mississippi for hundreds of years. It is the longest river in the United States.

Parts of western and southern Illinois are hilly, as well. Like northwest Illinois, these areas were not flattened by glaciers. Calhoun County in western Illinois has rugged, rolling **terrain**. So does southern Illinois. The Shawnee Hills of southern Illinois contain several hills that are more than 1,000 feet (305 meters) high. Southern Illinois is also home to Shawnee National Forest, the only national forest in the state. The ponderosa pine and Douglas fir trees of the forest blanket the hillsides. Most of the state, however, is a level plain about 600 feet (183 meters) above sea level.

More than 900 rivers and streams cross Illinois. Three large rivers form part of the state's borders. The Mississippi River forms the western border. The Ohio River is Illinois's southern border. The Wabash River makes up much of the state's eastern border. The Rock, Kaskaskia, Big Muddy, Illinois, and many other rivers run through the interior of the state. These rivers drain a large part of the middle United States. Water from 23 states flows through Illinois. Some flows eastward to the Atlantic Ocean, through Lake Michigan. Most flows south through the Ohio and Mississippi rivers to the Gulf of Mexico.

Illinois Topography

Illinois seems like mostly flatland at first, but each region actually has a variety of hills, fields, rivers, and lakes.

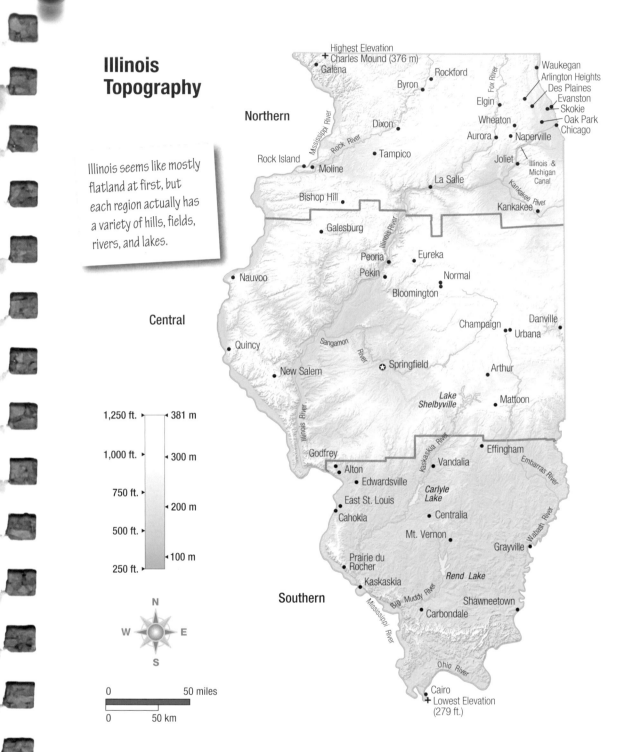

Northern

Highest Elevation
+ Charles Mound (376 m)
Galena
Byron
Rockford
Waukegan
Arlington Heights
Des Plaines
Evanston
Elgin
Skokie
Wheaton
Oak Park
Dixon
Aurora
Naperville
Chicago
Rock Island
Tampico
Joliet
Moline
Illinois & Michigan Canal
La Salle
Bishop Hill
Kankakee
Galesburg

Central

Peoria
Eureka
Pekin
Normal
Nauvoo
Bloomington
Quincy
Champaign
Danville
Sangamon River
Urbana
New Salem
Springfield
Arthur
Lake Shelbyville
Mattoon
Godfrey
Effingham
Alton
Vandalia
Edwardsville
Carlyle Lake
East St. Louis
Cahokia
Centralia
Mt. Vernon
Grayville
Prairie du Rocher
Rend Lake
Kaskaskia

Southern

Shawneetown
Carbondale
Cairo
+ Lowest Elevation (279 ft.)

1,250 ft.	381 m
1,000 ft.	300 m
750 ft.	200 m
500 ft.	100 m
250 ft.	

N
W E
S

0 — 50 miles
0 — 50 km

Illinois is home to both natural and artificial, or human-made, lakes. Most artificial lakes were created by building **dams** on rivers. Illinois's largest interior lake is Carlyle Lake, near Vandalia in southern Illinois. It covers 24,580 acres (9,947 hectares). Underground water supplies, or **aquifers**, are another important source of water for the state. Underground water is pumped up through wells and used to **irrigate** farm fields and for drinking.

Illinois at Work

Ancient glaciers left behind **minerals** that made Illinois's soil **fertile**. Today, Illinois is one of the nation's leading agricultural states. Corn and soybeans are the state's main crops. In fact, Illinois competes with Iowa for top ranking in U.S. corn and soybean production. Illinois farmers grow a variety of other crops as well. They grow wheat, asparagus, cabbage, green beans, apples, peaches, blueberries, and other fruits and vegetables.

Illinois is a leading hog-raising state. Illinois farmers also raise sheep, poultry, and cattle for both beef and dairy products. A few farms even raise exotic birds like **ostriches** and **emus** for their meat, hides, and feathers. Many of Illinois's agricultural products are sold to other countries, or **exported**. Illinois is second in the nation in the value of exported agricultural products. The state sends about 4 billion dollars worth of agricultural products overseas each year. Almost half the grain grown in Illinois each year is exported to other countries.

The Illinois Economy (2005)

Gross State Product (in dollars)

Finance, Insurance, & Real Estate	$124,175,000,000
Services	$95,984,000,000
Manufacturing	$74,826,000,000
Government	$54,666,000,000
Wholesale Trade	$38,871,000,000
Retail Trade	$32,833,000,000
Information	$20,858,000,000
Transportation & Warehouses	$20,144,000,000
Agriculture, Forestry, Fishing & Hunting	$2,071,000,000

Total Gross State Product in 2005: $560,032,000,000

The gross state product is the total value of the goods and services produced by the people of Illinois in a year. In 2005 Illinois produced over 560 billion dollars worth of goods.

The raising of livestock, such as hogs (below), is an important industry in Illinois. Illinois produces over 4 million head of hogs each year. Many hog farmers also grow corn, which they use to feed the hogs.

Beneath the surface of Illinois lie valuable **resources**. They include supplies of **petroleum**, **natural gas**, lead, and coal. Illinois has more **bituminous coal** beneath its surface than any other state. Coal is called a **fossil** fuel, because it comes from the fossilized remains of plants and animals buried more than 200 million years ago. It is also nonrenewable, which means once it runs out, we can't make more. Coal is burned to provide heat, which is used to run power plants that produce electricity.

The state's most valuable mineral resource is crushed stone. Other resources mined in Illinois include construction sand and gravel. Illinois is a leading producer of sand and gravel used by **industry**. Some Illinois sand is used to make glass. Illinois is also first in the production of **tripoli**, a rock used in the manufacturing of plastics and rubber. Illinois also produces clay and **limestone** used for building materials.

Ethanol

Corn and other Illinois farm produce is used as food, of course. However, crops are also turned into a wide variety of other products. These include soap, paint, ink, wax, paper, medicines, animal feed, and glue. One of the most important products made from Illinois crops is ethanol. Ethanol is a fuel, made from corn, that is used in gasoline to help power cars and trucks. The state produces 690 million gallons (2.6 billion liters) of ethanol each year.

Illinois Resources

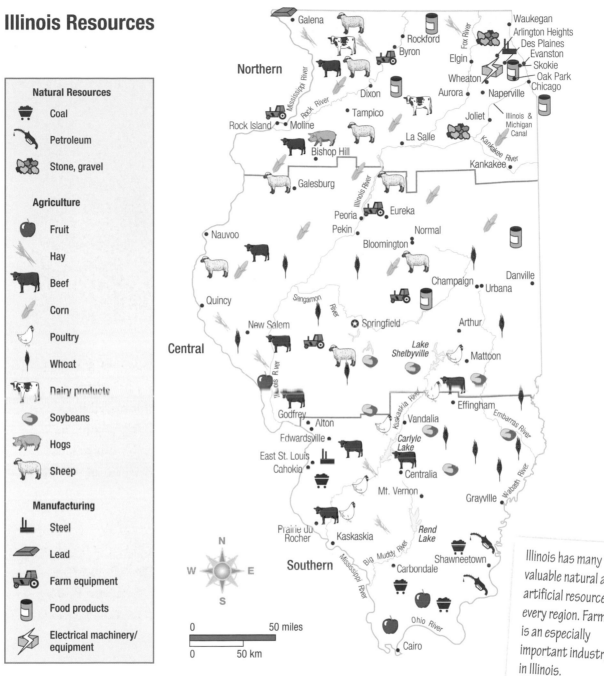

Natural Resources

- Coal
- Petroleum
- Stone, gravel

Agriculture

- Fruit
- Hay
- Beef
- Corn
- Poultry
- Wheat
- Dairy products
- Soybeans
- Hogs
- Sheep

Manufacturing

- Steel
- Lead
- Farm equipment
- Food products
- Electrical machinery/equipment

Northern

Central

Southern

Galena · Rockford · Byron · Waukegan · Arlington Heights · Des Plaines · Evanston · Skokie · Elgin · Oak Park · Chicago · Wheaton · Aurora · Naperville · Dixon · Tampico · Joliet · Illinois & Michigan Canal · Rock Island · Moline · La Salle · Bishop Hill · Kankakee · Galesburg · Peoria · Eureka · Pekin · Normal · Bloomington · Nauvoo · Danville · Champaign · Urbana · Quincy · Springfield · Arthur · New Salem · Lake Shelbyville · Mattoon · Godfrey · Alton · Vandalia · Effingham · Edwardsville · Carlyle Lake · East St. Louis · Cahokia · Centralia · Mt. Vernon · Grayville · Prairie du Rocher · Kaskaskia · Rend Lake · Shawneetown · Carbondale · Cairo

Mississippi River · Rock River · Fox River · Illinois River · Kankakee River · Sangamon River · Kaskaskia River · Embarras River · Wabash River · Big Muddy River · Ohio River

N · W · E · S

0   50 miles
0   50 km

Illinois has many valuable natural and artificial resources in every region. Farming is an especially important industry in Illinois.

Many of Illinois's industries are related to agriculture and mining. Since the 1830s, Illinois factories have made farm equipment. Illinois is home to more than 1,000 food producing companies that turn the state's crops into food. Illinois is a leading producer of flour, syrups, cooking oils, and pet food. Food processing is the state's top manufacturing industry. Illinois is also a leading producer of cellular phones, chemicals, radios, televisions, and printed materials. Many of these products are sold to consumers in other countries. Illinois is sixth among states in the value of its exported goods.

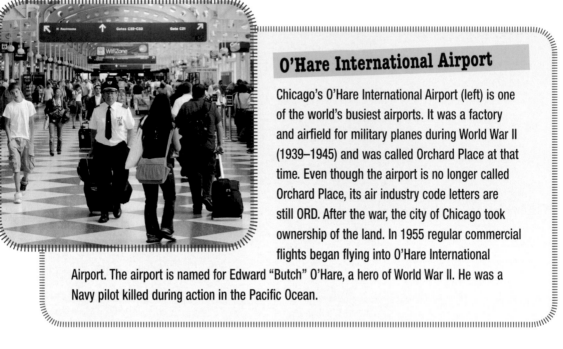

O'Hare International Airport

Chicago's O'Hare International Airport (left) is one of the world's busiest airports. It was a factory and airfield for military planes during World War II (1939–1945) and was called Orchard Place at that time. Even though the airport is no longer called Orchard Place, its air industry code letters are still ORD. After the war, the city of Chicago took ownership of the land. In 1955 regular commercial flights began flying into O'Hare International Airport. The airport is named for Edward "Butch" O'Hare, a hero of World War II. He was a Navy pilot killed during action in the Pacific Ocean.

Crossroads

Illinois has always been a crossroads state. It is located in the middle of the United States and near important waterways. Before trains, cars, and planes, water travel was the best way to move around. For thousands of years, Native Americans used the rivers and lakes of Illinois as highways. They paddled hundreds of miles to trade with distant neighbors. Today, large ships and **barges** travel up and down the Illinois, Mississippi, and Ohio rivers. They carry Illinois crops and goods to market.

In the late 1800s, Illinois became the world's greatest railroad center. Railroads from all over the country met in Illinois. Trains still carry people and products to and from Illinois. In fact, Illinois trains carry over 450 million tons (408 metric tons) of freight each year.

Hundreds of years ago, rivers carried travelers and goods to Illinois. Today, interstate highways do the job. Illinois has more than 2,000 miles (3,219 kilometers) of interstate highways.

Illinois Transportation

Illinois has many miles of highways and railroad tracks, as well as several airports. It is a center for transportation in the United States.

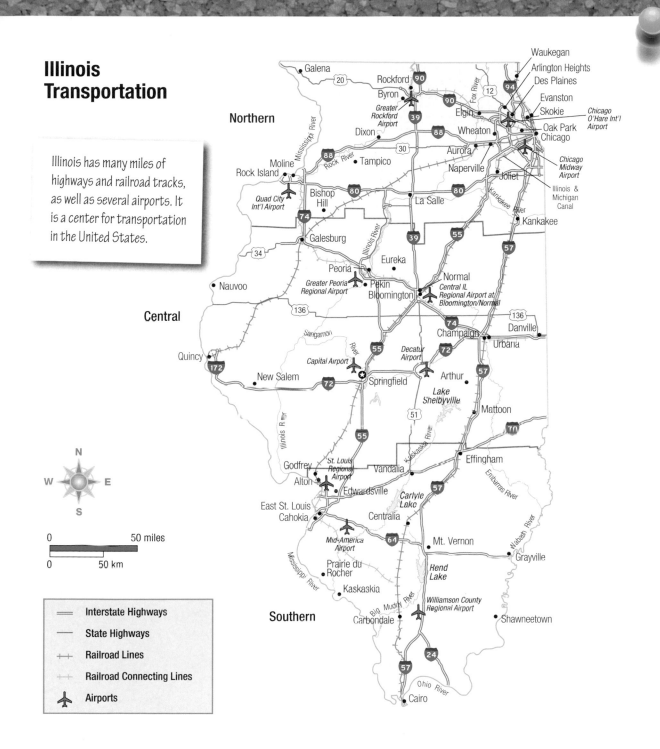

Legend:
- ═══ Interstate Highways
- ─── State Highways
- +++ Railroad Lines
- +++ Railroad Connecting Lines
- ✈ Airports

In the late 1900s, Illinois was the destination for more air travelers than any other place in the world. Chicago's O'Hare International Airport earned the title "world's busiest airport." More than 65 million travelers use O'Hare each year. Illinois is also home to over 100 public airports, as well as many landing strips.

State and interstate highways also connect Illinois to the world. Illinois is third in the country in interstate miles. It boasts more than 2,000 miles (3,219 kilometers) of interstate highways. It has another 34,000 miles (54,000 kilometers) of state highways.

Northern Illinois

The area that is now northern Illinois almost became part of Wisconsin. Before Illinois became a state in 1818, the United States Congress had to set Illinois's borders. Originally, Illinois's northern border was supposed to be near the southern tip of Lake Michigan. However, an Illinois leader named Daniel Pope Cook convinced Congress to redraw the map of the new state. Congress moved the border 41 miles (66 kilometers) north, to its present position. Cook County, Illinois, was named in Cook's honor.

The northwest part of the state is full of rolling hills (above), as well as the state's highest point: Charles Mound.

Chicago (below) is the state's largest city and the third largest in the country. It lies on the shores of Lake Michigan, one of Illinois's greatest resources.

The area of Illinois added by Congress became very important to the state's development. That area includes the beautiful Apple River Valley of northwest Illinois. It also includes most of Illinois's Lake Michigan shoreline. That shoreline helped connect Illinois to the rest of the Great Lakes and eastern United States. The northern region also includes Galena, the home of the 18th president of the United States, Ulysses S. Grant. It includes part of the Rock River Valley, the childhood home of Ronald Reagan, the 40th president of the United States. It also includes Chicago, by far the biggest city in the state and the third largest in the nation.

Land and Water

Northern Illinois includes the state's highest point. It is also home to some of the lowest-lying land in the state. In between are smaller hills, valleys, and bits of the **prairies** that once covered Illinois.

Illinois's highest point is Charles Mound in Jo Daviess County. It is located in the northwest corner of the state. This area is one of three "driftless areas" of Illinois, or areas that were never covered by **glaciers**. As a result, the land there has not been flattened by the actions of glaciers. Instead, it is marked by small but steep slopes.

Across the state, northeast Illinois has a very different natural history. It is the area of Illinois that was most recently covered by glaciers. The last of the glaciers melted away about 15,000 years ago. The melting water of that glacier formed a huge lake that covered the site where Chicago stands today. Eventually, the water drained away down ancient rivers to the Gulf of Mexico. Today, Chicago and other parts of northeast Illinois stand on what used to be the bed of that ancient lake. The land there is very flat and lower than other parts of Illinois. Some of Chicago was even built on what used to be swampland.

Northern Illinois contains Charles Mound, the highest point in the state at 1,235 feet (376 meters). It also contains hilly land, important rivers, the Lake Michigan shoreline, and Chicago.

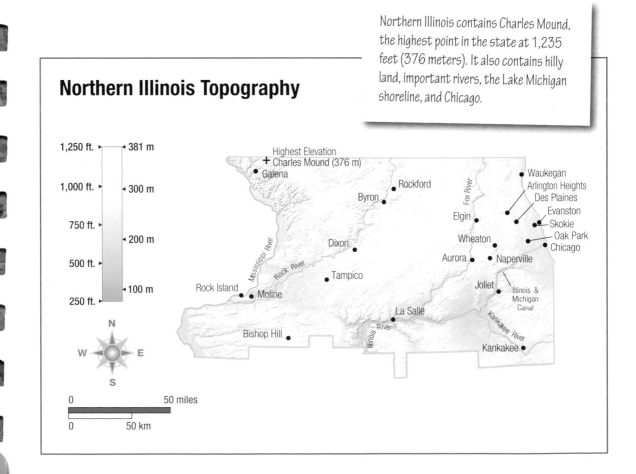

Northern Illinois Topography

1,250 ft.	381 m
1,000 ft.	300 m
750 ft.	200 m
500 ft.	
250 ft.	100 m

Highest Elevation
Charles Mound (376 m)
Galena
Byron
Rockford
Fox River
Waukegan
Arlington Heights
Des Plaines
Evanston
Elgin
Skokie
Wheaton
Oak Park
Chicago
Aurora
Naperville
Mississippi River
Rock River
Dixon
Tampico
Rock Island
Moline
Joliet
Illinois & Michigan Canal
La Salle
Kankakee River
Bishop Hill
Illinois River
Kankakee

N
W   E
S

0   50 miles

0   50 km

Midewin National Tallgrass Prairie

Much of northern Illinois was once home to vast prairies. Patches of prairie can still be found in the region. The Midewin National Tallgrass Prairie is one of the biggest prairie preserves in the state. A preserve is a place where **conservation** of the land and its **resources** is practiced. Midewin is located near Joliet, on the site of a former U.S. Army plant. It was replanted with native prairie grasses, similar to those that once covered Illinois. Today, it offers a glimpse of the kind of land that settlers in the early 1800s found in Illinois.

Much of north-central Illinois is flat, too. However, there are areas of gentle slopes and ridges. These ridges are called **moraines**. They are piles of ground-up rock and dirt left behind by glaciers. One of the largest moraines in Illinois is the Bloomington Moraine. It is a C-shaped ridge that runs from just north of DeKalb to just east of Bloomington.

Northern Illinois contains some beautiful river valleys. The Apple River Valley Canyon formed as waters of the Apple River cut through **limestone** over thousands of years. This process is called **erosion**. In a similar way, the Pecatonica River cut steep canyons that are up to 250 feet (76 meters) deep.

The Apple River Canyon (above) was formed by water from the Apple River cutting through limestone over thousands of years in a process called erosion.

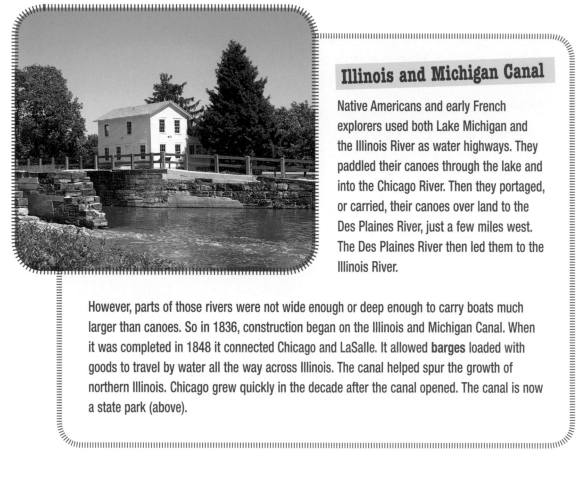

Illinois and Michigan Canal

Native Americans and early French explorers used both Lake Michigan and the Illinois River as water highways. They paddled their canoes through the lake and into the Chicago River. Then they portaged, or carried, their canoes over land to the Des Plaines River, just a few miles west. The Des Plaines River then led them to the Illinois River.

However, parts of those rivers were not wide enough or deep enough to carry boats much larger than canoes. So in 1836, construction began on the Illinois and Michigan Canal. When it was completed in 1848 it connected Chicago and LaSalle. It allowed **barges** loaded with goods to travel by water all the way across Illinois. The canal helped spur the growth of northern Illinois. Chicago grew quickly in the decade after the canal opened. The canal is now a state park (above).

Northern Illinois rivers have played an important role in the state's history. The Chicago and Des Plaines rivers were part of the route that carried French traders from Canada to the Mississippi River in the late 1600s. However, northern Illinois wasn't settled for about another 150 years. When settlers did come to the region, they settled along the rivers. In the early 1800s, steamboats on the Mississippi River began to serve the booming mining town of Galena. In the 1830s, settlers from New England and New York began to settle along the Fox and Rock rivers.

Canals also helped northern Illinois grow. In 1848 the Illinois and Michigan Canal opened between Chicago and LaSalle. This made it possible for boats and barges to travel across the state, from the Mississippi River to Lake Michigan. The canal helped make Chicago a center for Illinois trade. Today, the canal is a state park lined with nature preserves and historic sites.

Natural Resources

Many of northern Illinois's first settlers came to mine lead near Galena. The lead mines of northwest Illinois became one of the state's first **industries**. They also helped make Galena a successful town. One of the primary uses of lead was in the making of bullets.

Later, limestone **quarries** and clay pits across northern Illinois provided building materials for growing cities. Crushed stone and gravel from northern Illinois still help supply builders of roads and **suburbs**.

One of northern Illinois's greatest natural resources is underground water. Much of northern Illinois draws its drinking water from wells that bring water up from deep under the ground.

Northern Illinois has a wide variety of resources. The northwest corner has long been known as a source of lead. Most manufacturing takes place around the Chicago area.

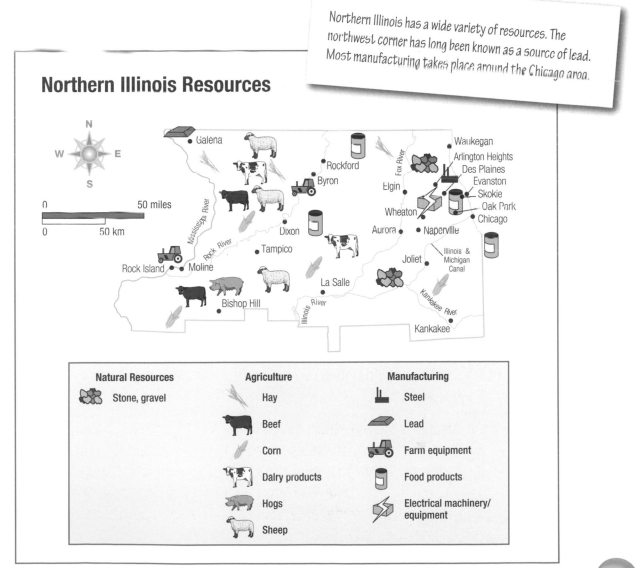

Northern Illinois Resources

Galena · Rockford · Byron · Dixon · Tampico · Rock Island · Moline · Bishop Hill · La Salle · Waukegan · Arlington Heights · Des Plaines · Evanston · Skokie · Oak Park · Chicago · Elgin · Wheaton · Aurora · Naperville · Joliet · Kankakee

Mississippi River · Rock River · Fox River · Illinois River · Kankakee River · Illinois & Michigan Canal

N W E S

0   50 miles
0   50 km

Natural Resources	Agriculture	Manufacturing
Stone, gravel	Hay	Steel
	Beef	Lead
	Corn	Farm equipment
	Dairy products	Food products
	Hogs	Electrical machinery/equipment
	Sheep	

Climate

Northern Illinois experiences cold, dry winters and warm, humid summers. Areas near Lake Michigan are the most humid during the summer months. Compared to other parts of Illinois, the north gets less yearly rainfall. About 34 inches (86 centimeters) of rain will fall in a typical year in northern Illinois. That compares to about 46 inches (117 centimeters) of rain in southern Illinois. Northern Illinois gets less rainfall because it is farther from the Gulf of Mexico. Much of the rainfall in Illinois begins as water vapor from the Gulf of Mexico that travels north in clouds. However, northern Illinois sees more snowstorms than other parts of the state. About 36 inches (91 centimeters) of snow fall during a typical winter.

Like other parts of the state, northern Illinois is hit by tornadoes. Tornadoes are rotating funnels of air that move from thunderstorm clouds to the ground. They are powerful enough to destroy buildings and property. Tornadoes have killed more than 1,000 people in Illinois since 1916.

Winter snowstorms can dump inches of snow in northern Illinois. Blizzards (above) can make getting around Chicago a more difficult experience.

Illinois Precipitation

The southern tip of Illinois gets the most rain each year. However, northern Illinois gets more snow than the rest of the state.

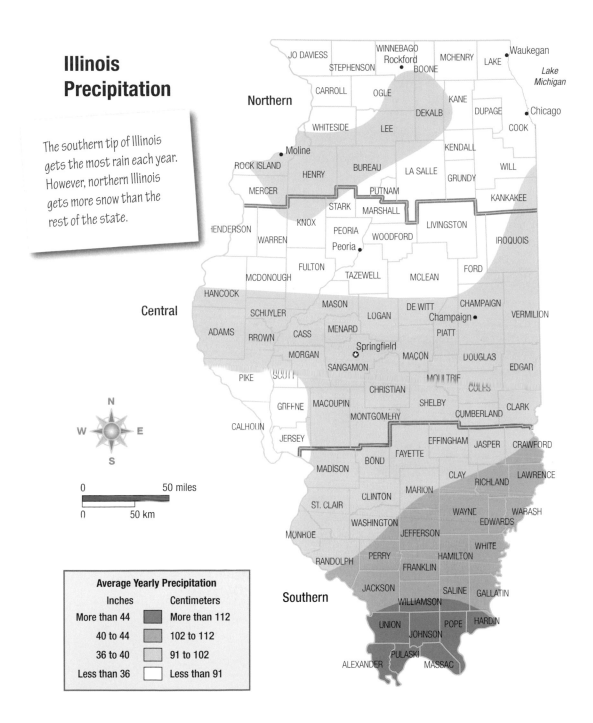

Northern

Central

Southern

JO DAVIESS · WINNEBAGO · Rockford · MCHENRY · LAKE · Waukegan · STEPHENSON · BOONE · Lake Michigan · CARROLL · OGLE · KANE · DUPAGE · DEKALB · Chicago · WHITESIDE · LEE · COOK · Moline · KENDALL · ROCK ISLAND · HENRY · BUREAU · LA SALLE · WILL · MERCER · PUTNAM · GRUNDY · KANKAKEE · STARK · MARSHALL · LIVINGSTON · KNOX · PEORIA · WOODFORD · IROQUOIS · HENDERSON · WARREN · Peoria · FORD · FULTON · TAZEWELL · MCLEAN · MCDONOUGH · HANCOCK · MASON · DE WITT · CHAMPAIGN · SCHUYLER · LOGAN · VERMILION · Champaign · MENARD · PIATT · ADAMS · BROWN · CASS · MORGAN · Springfield · MACON · DOUGLAS · EDGAR · PIKE · SCOTT · SANGAMON · MOULTRIE · COLES · CHRISTIAN · SHELBY · CLARK · GREENE · MACOUPIN · CUMBERLAND · CALHOUN · MONTGOMERY · JERSEY · EFFINGHAM · JASPER · CRAWFORD · FAYETTE · MADISON · BOND · CLAY · RICHLAND · LAWRENCE · CLINTON · MARION · WAYNE · WABASH · ST. CLAIR · WASHINGTON · EDWARDS · MONROE · JEFFERSON · WHITE · RANDOLPH · PERRY · HAMILTON · FRANKLIN · JACKSON · SALINE · GALLATIN · WILLIAMSON · UNION · POPE · HARDIN · JOHNSON · ALEXANDER · PULASKI · MASSAC

Average Yearly Precipitation

Inches	Centimeters
More than 44	More than 112
40 to 44	102 to 112
36 to 40	91 to 102
Less than 36	Less than 91

0 — 50 miles

0 — 50 km

The growing season in northern Illinois is about 155 days long, beginning in May and running until October. The growing season is the period during which an area experiences no frost. Frost is made of tiny droplets of ice that cover plants, often killing them. On a typical winter day in northern Illinois, the temperature is about 22° Fahrenheit (-6° Celsius). On a typical summer day, it's about 74° Fahrenheit (23° Celsius).

Industry

Illinois business and industry is dominated by Chicago and its suburbs. Chicago is the Midwest's leading financial center. It is the home of many banks, insurance companies, and companies that provide financial services. Chicago is also home to many manufacturing companies. Seven of every ten Illinois jobs in the manufacturing industry are in the Chicago area. The city and suburbs are leading producers of metal products and electronics. Chicago is the third largest center for printing and publishing in the United States. The Chicago area is also the home of some of the world's best-known food producers. Their products include baked goods from Sara Lee, Wrigley's chewing gum, and Kraft Foods. Many of the country's biggest companies have headquarters in Chicago or its suburbs. These include McDonald's, Sears Roebuck, United Airlines, Boeing, Quaker Oats, and Motorola.

This is a rare quiet moment at the Chicago Board of Trade at the end of La Salle Street in Chicago. Usually the area is bustling with traffic as traders work within. Chicago is the Midwest's leading financial center.

Of course, there are other business centers in northern Illinois. Rockford companies are leading producers of machine tools and auto parts. The Quad Cities of western Illinois are home to several companies that make farm equipment. The Quad Cities include Moline, East Moline, Rock Island, and Davenport, which is located just across the Mississippi River in Iowa. Deere and Company of Moline is one of Illinois's oldest businesses. It was founded in 1838 by John Deere, a **blacksmith** who invented the first successful steel plow.

Agriculture

Northern Illinois is home to Illinois's largest cities. However, most of the region is still covered by farms. Like other parts of the state, northern Illinois is a leading corn producer. Corn grown there is sold all over the United States and the world. Some of the corn is used as feed grain for farm animals. Fields of grass and clover in northern Illinois are turned into hay for farm animals. In Ogle and DeKalb counties, farmers also grow pumpkins.

Northern Illinois farmers also raise a variety of livestock animals. Sheep are raised in the hilly western sections for wool. Hogs and beef cattle are raised for meat and other products. Henry County is Illinois's leading hog producer. In the far northern sections of Illinois, dairy farms produce milk and cheese.

Harvard Milk Days

Harvard is the home of Harmilda, a life-size fiberglass cow that stands at the center of town. Harmilda (below) is named for Harvard Milk Days, a celebration held every year in June. It includes a parade and milk-drinking contests.

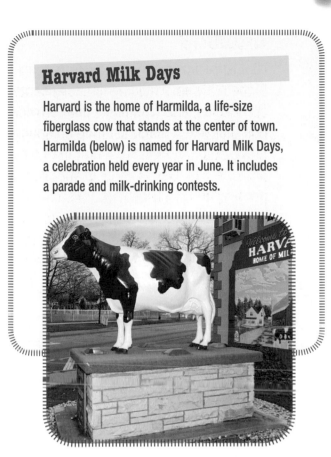

John Deere changed Illinois with the invention of his simple steel plow in 1838. Today, John Deere and Company makes more advanced farm machinery (below) in Moline. It is one of Illinois's oldest businesses.

Cities

Northern Illinois is home to eight of Illinois's ten largest cities. Chicago is by far the biggest city in Illinois. When Chicago became a city in 1833, it had just 350 residents. Sixty years later, Chicago's population was one million. After fifty years of declining populations, Chicago is growing again. In 2000 Chicago's population stood at 2,896,016. Chicago is world famous for its beautiful buildings and lakefront parks. It is also the Midwest's capital of business and industry. Chicago is second to New York City as a national financial hub.

Many of Chicago's suburbs are growing as well. Aurora has grown to become Illinois's third largest city. Its population is 142,990. Naperville is now the fourth largest city in Illinois, with 128,358 people. All around the Chicago area, new homes and businesses are being built on land that was once farmland. Major corporations like McDonald's and Baxter International have their headquarters in Chicago's suburbs. McDonald's restaurants are located in almost 120 countries around the world. Baxter International is a world leader in producing medicines and treatments for sick people.

Many of Chicago's suburbs are growing fast. People move from cities into new homes like these (below) partly to have more space, backyards, and garages. Today, suburban homes are often more affordable as well.

Rockford grew up around a ford—or place to cross a river—on the Rock River. Settlers built **mills** there that provided power for the city's furniture-making industry. Today, Rockford is Illinois's second largest city, with more than 150,000 people.

Rock Island, Moline, and East Moline are three of the four Quad Cities. (Davenport, Iowa, is the fourth.) The Quad Cities are located along either side of the Mississippi River. Rock Island was the site of the first railroad bridge across the Mississippi River, built in 1856.

Galena was Illinois's first **boomtown**. Area mines supplied much of the nation's lead in the 1830s and 1840s. (Galena is actually also the name of a kind of lead.)

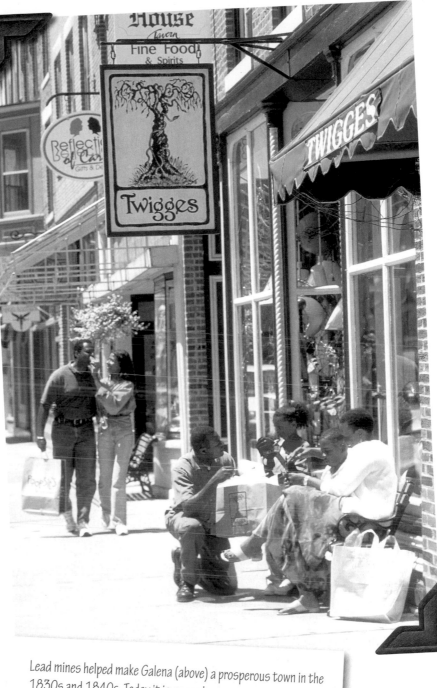

Lead mines helped make Galena (above) a prosperous town in the 1830s and 1840s. Today it is a popular tourist destination where people visit Grant's home and shop for antiques.

the name of a kind of lead.) The lead was shipped from Galena all over the country on steamboats that worked the Mississippi River. In the early 1800s, Galena was the richest town in Illinois. Today, people visit Galena to admire the city's grand old houses, shop for antiques, and visit the home of Ulysses S. Grant, Civil War general and the 18th president of the United States.

Central Illinois

Central Illinois has some of the world's richest farmland. It was once part of one of the largest **prairies** in the world. A person standing in the middle of the central Illinois prairie in the 1800s might see only tall grass in all directions. Many early pioneers compared it to being on a ship in the middle of the ocean. They called the prairie a sea of grass.

Central Illinois is no longer covered with tall prairie grass. Almost all of the prairies have been replaced by farms. The crops grown there are **exported** all over the world. Today, a person standing in a central Illinois field might see nothing but corn stalks in all directions.

However, visitors to central Illinois will also find scenic rivers lined with rocky **bluffs**. They will find lively cities and huge universities. And, on central Illinois's artificial lakes, they will see people boating and fishing.

Within 200 years, the vast prairies of central Illinois have been turned into vast fields of corn, soybeans, and other farm crops.

Peoria (below) is the oldest city in central Illinois. The French explorer La Salle built a fort near the site in the 1600s. Today, Peoria is the fifth most populated city in Illinois.

Land and Water

Central Illinois is the flattest part of the state. However, anyone who has ever tried to ride a bike there knows it's not perfectly flat. There are gentle slopes that rise to form ridges. These ridges are called **moraines**. They were formed by melting **glaciers** about 20,000 years ago. When the glaciers melted, they left behind piles of ground-up rock that formed the moraines. Several large moraines stretch across northern and central Illinois. Moraine View State Recreation Area is located on one of these moraines, just east of Bloomington.

Lake Shelbyville is one of the human-made lakes of central Illinois. Construction of a **dam** (above) there began in 1963. It was meant to control flooding in the area.

Between moraines there are stretches of low-lying land. During rainy periods, water can collect and turn the land into swampy bogs. Before this land could be successfully farmed, settlers had to drain it. They dug ditches that carried extra water away. In some parts of east-central Illinois, land was not fully drained for farming until around 1900.

Along the Mississippi River in central Illinois, the land becomes hilly. This was one of the few areas of Illinois that was not made flat by the actions of ancient glaciers. One of the hilly sections is in Calhoun County, between the Mississippi and Illinois rivers. Calhoun County sits on top of **karst** formations. Karst is **limestone** that is softened by water until it grows weak. Sometimes karst cracks and swallows trees and other parts of the landscape in large **sinkholes**.

Central Illinois's major rivers are the Kaskaskia, Illinois, Embarras, Vermillion, Mackinaw, and Sangamon. The first **forts** and trading posts built by French explorers in Illinois were along the Illinois River. After Illinois became a state in 1818, many early settlers lived along the rivers of central Illinois. On the riverbanks, they found timber for their fences and houses. They used the rivers themselves to float their farm produce to market on **flatboats**.

Central Illinois is home to few natural lakes. One of them, Lake Peoria, was the subject of cleanup efforts to rid it of pollution that was harming the wildlife. The central region has several human-made lakes. These include Lake Decatur and Lake Shelbyville.

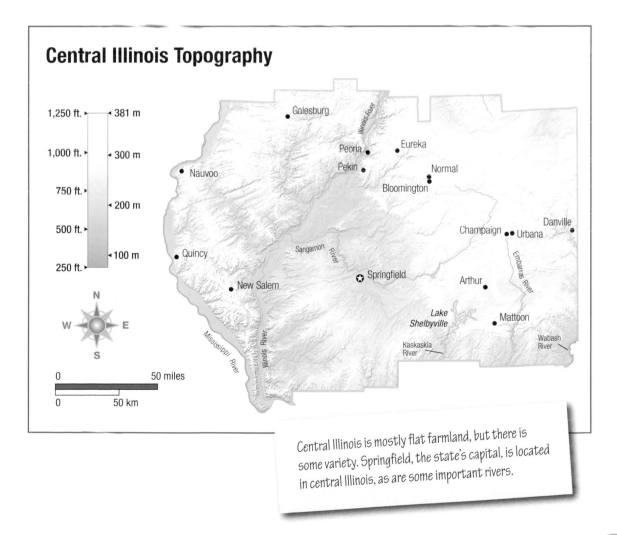

Central Illinois is mostly flat farmland, but there is some variety. Springfield, the state's capital, is located in central Illinois, as are some important rivers.

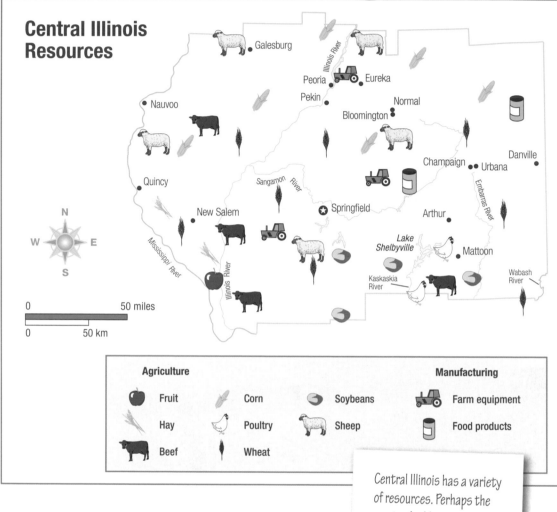

Central Illinois Resources

Agriculture
- Fruit
- Hay
- Beef
- Corn
- Poultry
- Wheat
- Soybeans
- Sheep

Manufacturing
- Farm equipment
- Food products

Central Illinois has a variety of resources. Perhaps the most valuable resource of the region is its farmland. Crops grown in central Illinois are sold all over the world.

Resources

Central Illinois's greatest **resource** is its rich farm soil. Beneath the soil, central Illinois also offers **mineral** resources. Limestone is gathered for use as a building material. Farmers also add limestone to some kinds of soil to make it more **fertile**. Some of Illinois's vast coal reserves are in central Illinois. So are the sand and gravel that are mined for use in building new homes and highways. Underground water is another valuable resource. Wells pumping water from under the ground provide much of Illinois's water. One of the challenges facing central Illinois is keeping its underground water supplies clean. Chemical **fertilizers** used in farming and waste from housing developments can seep through **porous** rock and pollute underground water.

Climate

Central Illinois experiences slightly warmer summers than northern Illinois. Its winters are slightly colder and snowier than southern Illinois. Central Illinois receives more freezing rainstorms than either southern or northern Illinois. See the map on page 21 to learn how much rain falls in central Illinois each year. On a typical January day in Springfield, the temperature will be 25° Fahrenheit (-4° Celsius). On a typical July day, it will be 76° Fahrenheit (24° Celsius). The growing season in central Illinois is 188 days long.

A "tornado belt" stretches across central Illinois, from Jersey County on the Mississippi River to Iroquois County on Illinois's eastern border. (It also extends along Lake Michigan in northern Illinois, and south along the Mississippi River in southern Illinois.) This stretch of land experiences the most tornadoes of any part of the state. A tornado that cut across central Illinois on May 26, 1917, killed 101 people. It was one of the ten deadliest tornadoes in Illinois history.

Central Illinois experiences more tornadoes than any other part of the state. Tornadoes can be very dangerous. They have killed more people in Illinois than in any other state.

Agriculture

The first settlers in central Illinois avoided the vast prairies. They thought the huge stretches of tall grass were a wasteland with no value for farming. The prairie land was very hard to prepare for planting. Farmers had to use cast-iron plows that didn't cut through the tough prairie grass roots. In 1838 John Deere invented a steel plow that could help farmers turn over prairie land. By 1847 the plows were being manufactured in Moline. They helped turn the great central Illinois prairie into valuable farmland. By 1900 most of the prairie had been replaced by farms.

The Military Tract

The western part of central Illinois is sometimes called the Military Tract. A tract is a piece of land. The Military Tract lies between the Illinois and Mississippi rivers. It includes Adams, Brown, Calhoun, Fulton, Hancock, Henderson, Knox, McDonough, Mercer, Peoria, Pike, Schuyler, Stark, and Warren Counties. Beginning in 1817, land there was divided up and given to veterans of the War of 1812 as a reward for their service. Some of the former soldiers came to Illinois to live on their new land. As a result, the western part of central Illinois was settled much earlier than the eastern part.

John Deere's new steel plow (left) helped farmers prepare the grassy soil of central Illinois for planting. It was able to cut cleanly through the tough roots of prairie grasses.

Corn has been a leading crop in Illinois since Native Americans began growing it 1,200 years ago. Today, McLean County in Illinois is the nation's leading corn-producing county.

In the late 1900s, Illinois farmers began growing soybeans, as well. Soybeans come from Asia originally and are used to make soy sauce, tofu, and other foods. They are also used to make products like ink and paint. Champaign County is the country's leading soybean producer.

Wheat is another leading crop, especially in Adams and Pike counties. Calhoun County is one of the few places in Illinois that grows peaches.

Industry

Industry in central Illinois is often connected to farming. Decatur is home to two large companies that process farm products. The A.E. Staley Company makes syrups and other products from corn. Archer Daniels Midland makes animal feed, fuel, and food products from corn, soybeans, and other Illinois crops.

In Peoria the Caterpillar Company makes trucks and tractors for farming and construction. The Keystone Steel Company in Bartonville began by making wire fences for farmers without easy access to wood. Today, it is a leading manufacturer of steel wire and rods.

Bloomington is home to State Farm Insurance and a large automobile plant. As the state capital, Springfield employs hundreds of people who work in the state government. The University of Illinois in Urbana-Champaign has long been a center of computer technology. The university helped develop a leading program used to explore the Internet.

The Caterpillar Company of Peoria is a leading manufacturer of farm equipment (above). It also makes equipment for construction, and is the largest employer in the Peoria area.

Cities

Bloomington and Normal sit in the center of Illinois at the junction of three interstate highways. The two cities are home to two of Illinois's oldest colleges. Illinois Wesleyan, in Bloomington, was founded in 1850. Illinois State University in Normal became Illinois's first state-supported college in 1857.

Urbana was founded in 1833. In 1854 the Illinois Central Railroad built a depot two miles west of town. Around that depot, the new city of Champaign quickly grew. The University of Illinois **campus** is spread across both towns. More than 30,000 students from all over the world study at the university.

Decatur calls itself the "Pride of the Prairie." It sits at the center of central Illinois's fertile farm region. In 1920 the A.E. Staley Company of Decatur began sponsoring a professional football team. They were called the Decatur Staleys. They later moved to Chicago and became known as the Chicago Bears.

The University of Illinois is one of the nation's largest state universities. Its main campus (above) is spread across the two towns of Champaign and Urbana in central Illinois.

Peoria's location on the Illinois River helped make it a shipping center for Illinois produce. Today, there are still old-fashioned paddleboats (below) on Peoria's waterfront, but they are used for fun cruises and special events.

French explorers built a fort near present-day Peoria in 1691. Some people claim this makes Peoria Illinois's oldest city. In fact, the city of Peoria wasn't founded until 1845. Because of its location on the Illinois River, Peoria became a shipping center for farm produce. Today, old-fashioned paddleboats can still be seen on Peoria's waterfront.

Springfield is Illinois's state capital. The capitol dome, completed in 1888, is a popular tourist destination. So are the many historic sites related to Abraham Lincoln, who lived in Springfield before he became president. In 2005 Springfield opened the new Abraham Lincoln Presidential Library and Museum.

Abraham Lincoln's former home in Springfield (above) is now a historic site operated by the National Park Service.

Southern Illinois

When some people think of Illinois, they think of cornfields. Others think of the skyscrapers of Chicago. Southern Illinois is a bit different. The ancient **glaciers** that flattened much of Illinois never reached the southern part of the state. As a result, southern Illinois has more steep hills, cliffs, and forests than any other part of Illinois.

A visitor enjoys the view from a rock outcropping at Garden of the Gods (above), which is located in the Shawnee National Forest at the southern tip of Illinois.

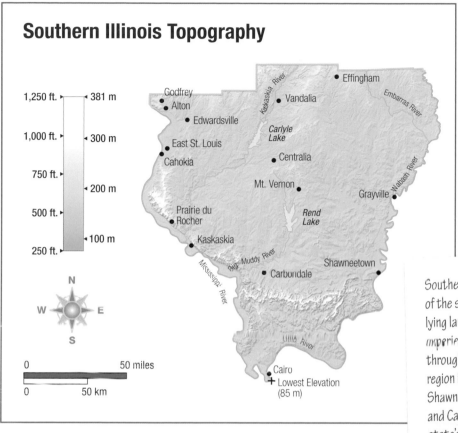

Southern Illinois Topography

1,250 ft. ► ◄ 381 m

1,000 ft. ► ◄ 300 m

750 ft. ► ◄ 200 m

500 ft. ► ◄ 100 m

250 ft. ►

N
W — E
S

0   50 miles

0   50 km

Godfrey
Alton
Edwardsville
Carlyle Lake
East St. Louis
Cahokia
Prairie du Rocher
Kaskaskia

Kaskaskia River
Vandalia
Centralia
Mt. Vernon
Rend Lake

Effingham
Embarras River
Grayville
Wabash River

Big Muddy River
Carbondale
Shawneetown
Mississippi River
Little River
Cairo
+ Lowest Elevation (85 m)

Southern Illinois has some of the state's lowest-lying land. The region has experienced severe floods throughout history. The region is home to the Shawnee National Forest and Carlyle Lake, the state's largest human-made lake.

Land and Water

Much of southern Illinois was once actually covered with forest. Settlers cut down those trees to build houses and fences for their farms. Only a small part of the original forest remains. However, some areas have remained forested. The Shawnee National Forest is home to some of the oldest and largest trees in the United States. It also has swamps that remind some visitors of southern states like Louisiana. The Shawnee National Forest is the only national forest in Illinois.

Parts of Monroe, Randolph, and St. Clair counties sit atop **karst** formations. These areas are marked by caves and **sinkholes**. In some places, water bubbles up from underground through springs.

Southern Illinois was the first part of the state to be settled. The French began building villages there around 1700. Around 1800, settlers from Kentucky and Tennessee began building farms along the area's rivers. Major rivers of southern Illinois include the Mississippi, Ohio, Embarras, Little Wabash, Muddy, and Kaskaskia. Southern Illinois has large human-made lakes that serve as a source of drinking water. Carlyle Lake, in the city of Carlyle, is Illinois's largest human-made lake. Rend Lake, near Mount Vernon, is Illinois's second-largest artificial lake. It was built in the late 1960s to serve as a water source for the surrounding area. It is also the center of Rend Lake State Fish and Wildlife Area, a wildlife **refuge**.

Coal mining has long been one of southern Illinois's most important industries. Illinois coal mines provide over 40 million tons (36 million metric tons) of coal each year. New technniques and technologies could help the coal industry survive in the future.

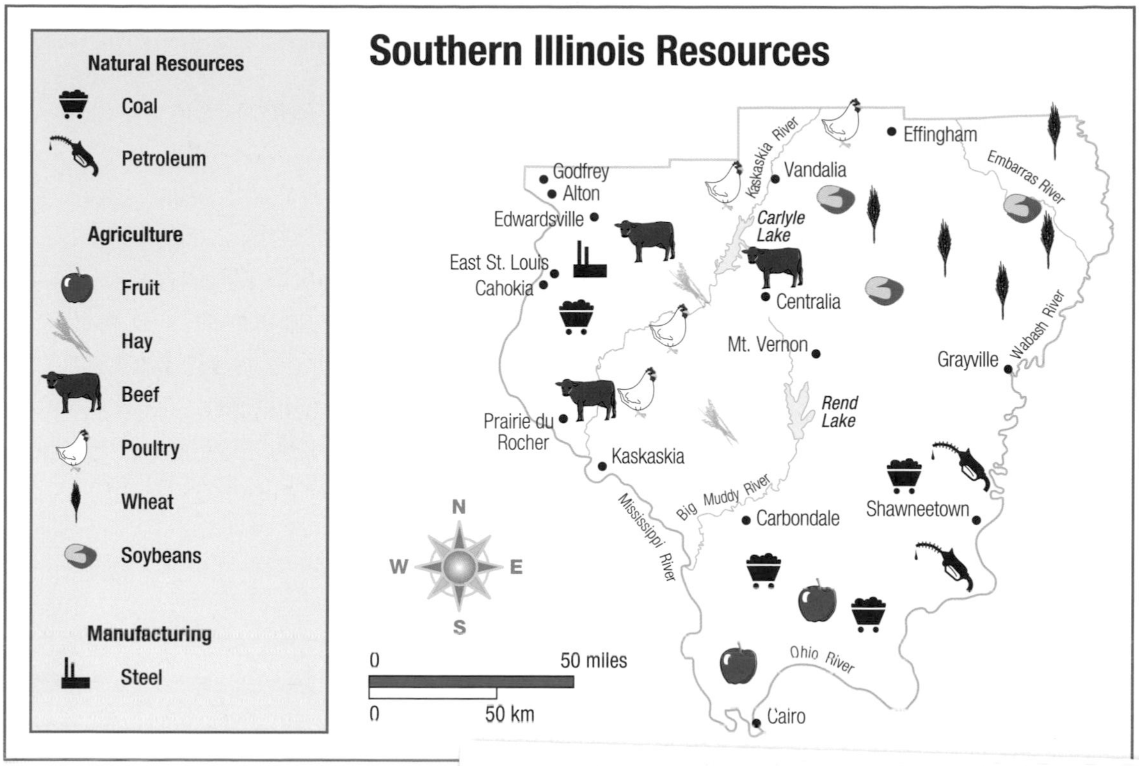
Southern Illinois Resources
Natural Resources
Coal
Petroleum
Agriculture
Fruit
Hay
Beef
Poultry
Wheat
Soybeans
Manufacturing
Steel
Effingham
Kaskaskia River
Vandalia
Godfrey
Alton
Edwardsville
Carlyle Lake
Embarras River
East St. Louis
Cahokia
Centralia
Mt. Vernon
Wabash River
Grayville
Prairie du Rocher
Rend Lake
Kaskaskia
Big Muddy River
Mississippi River
Carbondale
Shawneetown
Ohio River
Cairo
N
W
E
S
0
50 miles
0
50 km

Hay and wheat are important crops grown in southern Illinois. The climate and land of southern Illinois is also good for growing grapes. There are vineyards in the area around the Shawnee National Forest.

Resources

Southern Illinois is home to most of the state's coal. The first coal mines in the area opened in 1811, even before Illinois was a state. In the late 1800s, coal was used to power trains. Illinois produced a great amount of the coal at that time. Today, coal is used to run some of the plants that produce electric power. However, Illinois's **bituminous coal** is high in sulfur, which pollutes the air when it is burned. Laws require companies that burn high-sulfur coal to scrub it clean so it doesn't pollute the air. That process is so expensive that many companies choose not to use high-sulfur coal. However, new and improved mining techniques are making it less expensive to mine Illinois coal. Scientists are also working on new ways to burn coal without polluting the environment. At the start of the 21st century, new coal mines were once more opening in southern Illinois.

Most of the state's oil supply lies underneath southern Illinois as well. Thousands of Illinois oil wells reach deep underground to find oil. Parts of southern Illinois sit atop a foundation of **limestone**. Limestone is gathered for use as a building material. Farmers also add ground limestone to some kinds of soil to make it more **fertile**. Limestone is found in Monroe County, Randolph County, and parts of St. Clair County.

Climate

Southern Illinois enjoys much milder winters than do other parts of the state. On a typical January day in Cairo, the temperature will be 33° Fahrenheit (0.5° Celsius). Southern Illinois also receives fewer snowstorms than the rest of the state. Each year, southern Illinois receives about 10 inches (25 centimeters) of snow. However, summer temperatures can be quite warm, though the average is 74° Fahrenheit (23° Celsius). The growing season in southern Illinois is the longest in the state. It lasts about 210 days.

Throughout history, southern Illinois has been hit by destructive floods. In 1937 an Ohio River flood covered almost all of Gallatin County. Shawneetown was destroyed and had to be rebuilt on higher ground. In 1993 a Mississippi River flood destroyed Valmeyer in Monroe County. That town also had to be rebuilt on higher ground. See the map on page 21 to find out how much rain falls in southern Illinois each year.

Kaskaskia

Kaskaskia was Illinois's first state capital. It was built on fertile ground between the Kaskaskia and Mississippi rivers. It was an ideal spot for early settlers. However, Kaskaskia's location proved to be a bit dangerous. Only a sliver of land separated the two rivers. During storms, the rivers' currents would tear away chunks of land. Floods destroyed parts of Kaskaskia in 1844 and 1881. With each rainy season, more of Kaskaskia was lost. Eventually, the Mississippi River completely covered the neck of land separating it from the Kaskaskia River. As a result, the Mississippi River changed its course, so that it ran east of town. Today, Kaskaskia is the only part of Illinois that is west of the Mississippi River.

This farm north of Valmeyer was swallowed in a flood in 1993 (below). Floods that year damaged many Mississippi River towns. The low-lying land of southern Illinois, along with the rivers within and around it, make the region vulnerable to severe flooding.

Agriculture

Southern Illinois farmers grow some crops not found in other parts of the state. Illinois's biggest wheat-growing area is in southwestern Illinois. Southern Illinois farmers also raise livestock like hogs, poultry, and dairy cows. There are even several aquaculture farms in the ponds and rivers of southern Illinois. Aquaculture is the raising of fish for use as a food source.

Union County in southwestern Illinois produces apples and strawberries. Southern Illinois also produces grapes. The area around the Shawnee National Forest is home to several vineyards, where wine is made from grapes. In fact, the rough **terrain** of southern Illinois is perfect for grapes.

Orchards (right) in southern Illinois produce apples, which are the most valuable fruit crop in Illinois. Other fruits, such as grapes and strawberries, are grown in southern Illinois.

Egypt

The southern tip of Illinois is sometimes called "Egypt." The floods of the Ohio and Mississippi rivers make the land there fertile. This reminded early settlers of stories of the Nile River in Egypt. Many southern Illinois towns are named after places in Egypt, including Cairo, Thebes, and Karnak. The sports teams of Southern Illinois University are called the Salukis, named after a type of dog originally bred in ancient Egypt.

The Metro East cities are just across the Mississippi River from St. Louis, Missouri. The St. Louis Arch is visible from the Illinois side of the river (above).

Industry

Coal mining has long been one of southern Illinois's leading **industries**. However, the bituminous coal of Illinois contains large amounts of sulfur, a chemical that pollutes the air. Laws require that sulfur be removed from coal before it is burned for fuel. The costs of removing sulfur make Illinois coal very expensive to buy. In the 1980s and 1990s, many companies began buying less expensive coal from other states. As a result, many southern Illinois coal mines shut down. This forced thousands of workers to look for jobs in other fields. At the start of the 21st century, new coal-mining technologies offered hope that southern Illinois's coal mining industry would become strong again.

The Metro East area is home to many manufacturing plants. The Metro East area is the part of Illinois that contains **suburbs** of St. Louis, Missouri, which is located across the Mississippi River to the west. Metro East includes St. Clair, Madison, Monroe, Clinton, and Jersey counties. The Olin Company of East Alton makes metal for U.S. and foreign coins. It also produces metal for auto parts. Laclede Steel and U.S. Steel in Alton are also leading producers of metals.

Two State Fairs

Illinois has two state fairs. The Illinois State Fair in Springfield has been held every year since 1853. It offers agricultural exhibits, entertainment, and a life-size cow made of 500 pounds (227 kilograms) of butter. The DuQuoin State Fair dates back to 1923. One of its main attractions is harness racing (right), an event in which horses pull people in small carriages. Today, both fairs are operated by the state of Illinois.

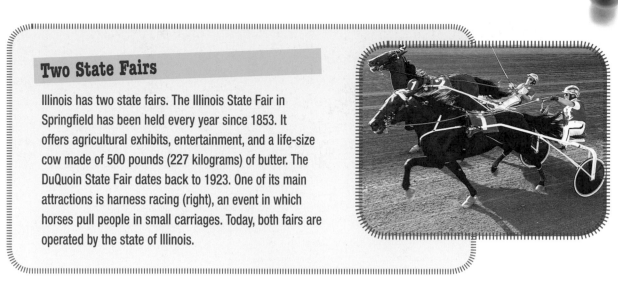

Transportation has long been one of southern Illinois's biggest businesses. Alton and other river cities were important shipping points for farm produce and industrial goods in the 1800s. Some of Illinois's first paved roads were built in southern Illinois in the late 1800s. Today, southern Illinois is serving air travelers at the huge Mid-America Airport in Mascoutah. It serves fliers going to and from St. Louis and its suburbs.

U.S. Steel (right) in Alton, Illinois, is a leading producer of flat, rolled, sheet steel. It is the largest business in Granite City and employs 3,100 people. U.S. Steel especially thrived at the end of the 1800s and in the early 1900s. During those years, many immigrants came from Central Europe to work in the Granite City steel industry.

Cave-in-Rock State Park

Cave-in-Rock State Park (below) is named for a cave on the Ohio River. In the early 1800s, the cave was a base for river pirates who preyed on pioneer travelers. Today, it is part of a 204-acre (82.5-hectare) park featuring hills, woods, and rugged cliffs. However, the river pirates are long gone.

Cities

Metro East is the second most populous area in the state, after the Chicago area. Metro East includes all of southern Illinois's largest cities, including Alton, Belleville, East St. Louis, and Granite City. The area is called Metro East because it is just east of St. Louis, Missouri, across the Mississippi River.

Alton's natural harbor made it a center for steamboat traffic on the Missouri and Mississippi rivers during the 1830s. Today, it is home to steel plants and other **industrial** businesses. The Lovejoy Memorial is one of Alton's historic sites. It pays tribute to Elijah Lovejoy, a newspaper publisher who campaigned against slavery in the 1830s. He was killed by a pro-slavery mob in 1837.

Belleville is the seat of St. Clair County. The county seat is the town in which a county's government is located. The first macadam road in Illinois ran from Belleville to East St. Louis in 1846. Macadam is a kind of road pavement made of crushed rock. Today, Belleville is at the connecting point of seven state highways. Scott Air Force Base is 9 miles (14.5 kilometers) east of Belleville.

Granite City was founded in 1896. In the early 1800s, the area was known as Six Mile **Prairie**. Farmers there traveled 6 miles (9.5 kilometers) to St. Louis to sell their produce. Granite City is now an industrial town, home to U.S. Steel and American Steel Foundries.

Cairo is the southernmost city in Illinois. Union troops were stationed there during the Civil War (1861–1865). More than one million Union soldiers passed through Cairo on their way to battlefields. Fort Defiance State Park in Cairo provides a view of the meeting of the Ohio and Mississippi rivers, which form the state borders at that point.

Cairo sits at the junction of the Ohio and Mississippi rivers (below). Those large rivers have carried people and goods to and from Illinois for hundreds of years.

Glossary

aquifer underground place containing water that can be reached by wells

barge large boat with a flat bottom, for carrying goods on rivers or canals

bituminous coal softer kind of coal that is dug from the ground and burned for fuel. Bituminous coal contains more carbon than some other types and has a high heating value.

blacksmith person who makes iron objects by heating them and hammering them on an anvil. Blacksmiths often make horseshoes.

bluff high, steep cliff

boomtown city that grows quickly

campus land around a college

conservation act of preserving or maintaining

dam wall built across a river to block the flow of water

emu large, flightless bird native to Australia

erosion process by which the surface of the earth is slowly worn away by wind or water

export sell goods to other countries; a good sold to other countries

fertile rich, productive

fertilizer substance that helps make soil more productive

flatboat boat with a flat bottom used for transporting goods in shallow waters

fort strong building used for defense against enemy attack

fossil remains or traces of a living thing of long ago

glacier large sheet of ice that spreads very slowly over land

industrial having to do with industries

industry kind of business

irrigate supply crops with water by digging human-made streams

karst area of land made up of softened limestone

limestone type of rock used as a building stone

mill building where grain is ground into flour

mineral solid substance formed in the earth by nature and obtained by mining

moraine ridge made of rocks and clay left behind by glaciers

natural gas mixture of gases found naturally in the earth and taken out through pipes to be used for fuel

ostrich large, flightless bird

petroleum similar to oil; oily liquid found in the earth in certain layers of rock

porous full of small holes

prairie large area of flat land with a lot of grass and very few trees

quarry pit from which stone or gravel is taken

refuge place offering protection from danger

resource something that is available to take care of a need; there are natural and human-made resources

sinkhole hole formed in rock by the action of water

suburb city or town just outside a larger city; suburban means having to do with a suburb

terrain land

tripoli light-colored rock often used for polishing metals and stones

wetlands land with wet and spongy soil

Find Out More

Further Reading

Bial, Raymond. *The Farms: Building America*. Tarrytown, NY: Marshall Cavendish, 2002.

Bowden, Rob. *Settlements of the Mississippi River*. Chicago: Heinemann Library, 2005.

Brown, Vanessa. *Illinois*. New York: Rosen, 2006.

Kummer, Patricia K. *One Nation: Illinois*. Mankato, MN: Capstone, 2003.

Oxlade, Chris. *Storm Warning: Tornadoes*. Chicago: Raintree, 2005.

Sutcliffe, Jane. *John Deere*. Minneapolis, MN: Lerner, 2007.

Ylvisaker, Anne. *Lake Michigan*. Mankato, MN: Capstone, 2005.

Websites

http://www.agr.state.il.us/about/agfacts.html
This site, from the Illinois Department of Agriculture, provides information and a link for kids, with fun facts about farming in the state.

http://www.historyillinois.org/hist.html
This Illinois history resource page provides links to many sites about the people of Illinois, as well as the state's government, history, and symbols.

http://www.illinois.gov/facts/history.cfm
This Illinois government-run site features amazing historical facts about the state. It covers 1673 to the present.

Index